Tools for Teaching and Training

TOOLS
FOR TEACHING
AND TRAINING

LeRoy Ford

BROADMAN PRESS • *Nashville, Tennessee*

Library of Congress catalog card number 61-5630
Printed in the United States of America
3.5O6513

Preface

The *tools for teaching and training* described here are simply "idea germs" which may be adapted by the creative teacher, whether he be in religious or secular education. The application of some of the illustrations pertains to classroom lesson presentation; others pertain to church administration, teacher training, and discussion groups. Regardless of the immediate application, the material is presented basically in the form of ideas for exploitation.

Because the field of simplified learning aids is largely undeveloped, some terms used have been coined by the writer. Some commonly used terms have been discarded because of the limitations they imply, and more inclusive terms have been adopted.

I wish to express my appreciation to those whose counsel and encouragement have contributed to the results of these efforts. To Dr. W. R. Fulton, associate professor of education, Oklahoma University, go my thanks for deepening my interest in the field of simple learning aids. To Dr. Raymond M. Rigdon, Editor-in-chief, Training Union Lesson Courses, Baptist Sunday School Board, go my thanks for suggesting that this material be prepared. To Mr. Bartlett Dorr, Mr. Frank Armstrong, and Mr. James Whaley go my thanks for some of the suggestions included here. Special appreciation is due Dr. E. F. Hallock and the First Baptist Church, Norman, Oklahoma, for providing me the opportunity to test these suggestions through actual use in a program of religious education. An expression of appreciation is due my wife for her help in preparing the manuscript.

LEROY FORD

Contents

1

Recognition of Principles

Teaching is a fine art. It involves the taking of things that are known to fashion a creative product. A full-grown Christian does not just happen. He is the result of a joint enterprise. As an individual is placed in the hands of a teacher and the Master Teacher, he is invested with new form and begins to grow toward the standard of perfection exemplified in Jesus. He begins to appropriate the privileges he has as a creation in the image of God.

Develop a Teaching Plan

The creative teacher will recognize some basic principles as he seeks to develop his teaching plan.

By finding out what a pupil needs and how he learns, the teacher can know what to teach and how to teach.

What the pupil needs.—Though pupils have many different and definite needs, all of them are but composites of one basic need. That need is spiritual maturity.

How the pupil learns.—The pupil learns from his experiences. These are both direct and indirect, and include learning through divine revelation. The learner cannot learn all he needs to know by direct experience. Herein lies the significance of the ideas presented in the following chapters. These ideas are designed to facilitate learning through indirect experiences.

Generally, experiences are impressed through the five senses—sight, hearing, touch, smell, and taste. The pupil learns best when

9

an activity involves a combination of senses. Suggestions included in the succeeding chapters employ the sense of sight, to which the teacher is to add an audible explanation, thus making a "multi-sensory" presentation.

What to teach.—A teacher does not teach lessons—but pupils. Nevertheless, he must teach the pupil *something*. The pupils' needs indicate that they must be taught the eternal truth of the gospel as revealed in the Word of God. The salvation of every pupil and the growth of that pupil toward Christian maturity should be the aim of all teaching.

How to teach.—The creative teacher teaches in many ways. In the final analysis, the teacher's personal being is his most influential method of teaching and aid to learning. In maintaining a deep devotional and prayer life, praying that the Holy Spirit will use him and what he says and does to teach the lessons which he himself cannot teach, the teacher has taken the major step toward application of effective methods.

The creative teacher also considers all the means and methods available to him, basing the methods on sound teaching principles. Recognizing that effective planning precedes effective learning experiences, he follows the logical steps in lesson planning and programing. These steps include:

1. Select an appropriate aim.
2. Relate the lesson or program to the unit of which it is a part.
3. Select the best methods of presentation.
4. Prepare suitable learning aids.
5. Follow through with carry-over activities.
6. Evaluate the results.

The purpose of this book is to help the teacher in taking one of the steps listed, namely, "Prepare suitable learning aids." Discussion of the other steps is left to other books and publications.

The number of direct experiences necessary for learning decreases in proportion to the number and effectiveness of direct experiences the learner has had. Direct experiences make it possible for words and other symbols to take on meaning for the learner. This fact explains why most of the learning aids described in succeeding chapters are most effective when used with Adults, Young People, Intermediates, or Juniors. Boys and girls in children's age groups have not had a sufficient background of direct experiences to make word symbols take on meaning.

No learning aid is of itself either effective or ineffective. It becomes so as the skill of the teacher and the quality of material rise above or fall below acceptable standards. A skilled teacher is not only an artist in creating materials but he is an artist in understanding individual differences. He will choose one method to use in teaching a child and perhaps another in teaching an adult. "The same materials may be used by two teachers having identical aims, but the results will vary according to the skill with which the instruction is given."[1]

Imperfect art may have more teaching value than that which is artistically perfect. This principle is important for the teacher who designs his own teaching aids. The idea is credited to George Froebel, who was one of the world's great educators. It leaves the unartistic teacher without excuse in developing creative teaching aids.

Use Simple Learning Aids

The use of simple learning aids in teaching, though not as effective as the use of direct experiences, is extremely effective. There are many sound reasons for their use.

Learning aids can attract attention.—"The first essential of teaching is the securing of attention."[2] Leaders and teachers often attract the attention of the pupil through use of a striking illustration, a thought-provoking question, or the employment of unusual activities. Attention may also be attracted through the use

---

[1] George H. Fickes, *Principles of Religious Education* (New York: Fleming H. Revell Co., 1937), p. 14.

[2] Gaines S. Dobbins, *Teaching Adults in the Sunday School* (Nashville: Broadman Press, 1936), p. 95.

of learning aids. A hidden chalkboard chart, on which points in an outline are hidden by strips of paper, will attract attention. It will not teach the lesson but it will help prepare the pupil. A resource center, consisting of books and objects related to a subject under consideration, will attract attention. It will help the pupil feel that the teacher or leader has prepared. He begins to feel that the presentation will be of value to him.

Learning aids can hold attention.—Attention at the beginning of a program does not prove that it will last throughout the period. Attention is temporary. It must be attracted and reattracted. Learning aids, creatively designed, can be used throughout a discussion or teaching period. The hidden chalkboard chart, for example, can help the teacher hold the attention of the group because not all of the chart is used at the same time. The "hidden" portions of the outline make the chart, in reality, a

Fig. 1—The Same Words May Mean Different Things to Different People

series of charts, each of which can be used at the appropriate time in a presentation.

Learning aids, especially objects, can help to make learning uniform.—This is especially important when teaching children whose vocabulary is limited. Sometimes the same words mean different things to different people (see Fig. 1).

Learning aids can help the leader time his presentation.—It is not enough to *present* an idea through use of a learning aid. The idea ought to be presented at the *time* the pupil is ready to receive it. The alert teacher is in a good position to know or sense the pupils' readiness to go from one step to another in the sequence of lesson presentation. The learning aid supplements the teacher's knowledge of subject matter, method of discussion, and understanding of the pupil and helps make effective the teaching-learning process which evolves from this knowledge and understanding.

Learning aids can set the stage for deepening of interest.—Aids of themselves cannot create interest. Interest is the connecting link between an idea and the pupil. It is created when the pupil associates the idea with a need he feels or may become aware of. Learning aids can form an initial point of contact from which the leader may proceed from the known to the unknown in the pupil's experience.

Learning aids can help to increase retention on the part of the pupil.—Learning aids, supplemented by the teacher's voice, make the learning experience "multi-sensory." An aid which has attracted and is holding attention, and which at the same time is being explained verbally by the leader, appeals to both the sense of sight and the sense of hearing. A learning aid which is manipulated by the pupil himself makes learning even more effective. An appeal to more than one of the senses at the same time results in retention of more information over a longer period of time.

Learning aids can create anticipation.—If the pupil sees a learning aid which, because of its design, tells him that there are four points in an outline, but he can only see the first point, he begins to "ready" himself for the presentation of the next point.

Learning aids can serve as tools for preview and review.— Retention depends to a great extent upon repetition. An idea "planted" in a preview may develop during the presentation of the lesson and in the interval between preview and presentation. The idea may then be "clinched" in subsequent reviews and reminders which should lead to application of the idea in a life situation.

Learning aids can be used to show relationships.—The human mind cannot comprehend all the facets of a problem or idea at the same time. Learning aids make it possible for the teacher or leader to develop the presentation of an idea in logical sequence. When a learning procedure extends over several days or weeks, relationships between the segments of the unit can be related to each other and to the basic unit idea through the use of learning aids.

The pages which follow present descriptions, illustrations, and suggestions for the use of charts, maps, chalkboard, posters, and other special devices. Most of the material pertains to the great variety of charts which may be used in teaching. The last chapter discusses briefly some principles of selecting learning aids as they relate to lesson or program units.

2

Charts

Charts are visual symbols for summarizing, comparing, contrasting, or performing other services in explaining subject matter.[1]

The creative teacher can vary the design of charts to increase their effectiveness. Perhaps no device is more adaptable to more situations than the chart. It is especially adaptable in relating lessons or programs to the unit as a whole and in relating parts of a lesson or program to the whole. Charts may be generally classified as single charts (including hidden charts), flip charts, and clingcharts (discussed in chap. 3).

Single Charts

A single chart is a one page chart which may or may not make use of embellishments. The many types of hidden charts are included in this classification. Single charts will be discussed here under the designations of pin-board charts, sentence holder charts, embellished charts, single chart series, and hidden charts. Hidden charts include such types as the hinged chart, folded word strip chart, strip chart, and the slip chart.

Pin-board charts.—The pin-board chart is a chart consisting of consecutive word strips resting on pins or tacks stuck into a backing. It may be built a line at a time or used as a hidden

---

[1]Edgar Dale, *Audio-Visual Methods in Teaching* (Rev. Edition; New York: The Dryden Press, 1954), p. 325.

15

chart by turning the word strips backward to be exposed at the appropriate time. These charts make use of a sturdy backing such as fiberboard, cork, or heavy poster board.

Word strips may be cut from left-over cardboard or blank areas of old posters. Printing may be done with crayon, chalk, felt-point pens, Speedball pens, various available lettering guides and pens, or even with a partially dry shoe polish dauber.

The background may be used over and over again since it is not used for printing area. The size or shape of the backing is

FIG. 2—THE PIN-BOARD CHART

not of great importance; however, it is generally agreed that a rectangular shape in a 2:3 or 5:7 ratio is most acceptable. "The ancient Greek idea was that the most pleasing rectangle was one the sides of which were in the ratio of approximately 5:8. An oblong of this ratio is called the 'golden section,' and the golden ratio, whether it refers to a rectangle or an oval, is now generally accepted as the most pleasing to the eye."[2]

Although the pin-board chart is generally used for displaying

---

[2] Arthur Judson Brewster, Herbert Hall Palmer, and Robert G. Ingraham, *Introduction to Advertising* (New York: McGraw-Hill Book Co., Inc., 1954), p. 228.

word strips, it can be used effectively to display a picture or a series of pictures. If pictures from papers and magazines are used, they should be mounted on cardboard to facilitate handling.

Sentence holder charts.—The sentence holder chart is a chart on which word strips are held in paper channels. Some of these charts are available commercially, but they may be constructed from simple materials. A semi-rigid backing is necessary. Cut several narrow strips of cardboard one-half inch wide. Stick a strip on a margin of adhesive tape one inch wide, leaving an uncovered area of the tape at each end. Stick the tape and strip of cardboard to the backing, making a pocket at the top. Word

FIG. 3—SENTENCE HOLDER CHART

strips can then be held securely in place by slipping them into the pockets.

The pockets may be used to hold a flat picture if it has a rigid backing. Large pictures may be placed in the lower pocket of the chart. A series of pictures may be used if they are small enough to fit between the pockets.

Embellished charts.—An embellished chart is a single chart which makes use of an embellishment to attract attention or point out information. All points on the chart are visible at the same time but the embellishment calls special attention to specific points. An embellishment is a component part designed to extend beyond the borders of the chart or to create a three-dimensional effect. Adhesive is placed on the back of the embellishment so that it will adhere to the backing and may be moved when the teacher desires. Effectiveness can be increased by making the embellishment from bright colored paper. When not in use, the embellishment can be placed in an inconspicuous place at the top or back of the chart.

FIG. 4—EMBELLISHED CHART

Single chart series.—The single chart series consists of several single charts which may be stacked, unbound, on an easel. The top chart may be removed to reveal the next. As charts are used, they may be stacked on the floor or placed at the back of the stack. In either case they are automatically stacked in order and are ready for reuse.

Hidden charts

A hidden chart is any of several types of single charts which may be hidden and revealed wholly or in parts to make possible appropriate timing of a presentation. Hidden charts are discussed here as hinged charts, folded word strip charts, strip charts, and slip charts.

Hinged charts.—The hinged chart is a hidden chart on which word strips, secured with a tape hinge, may be flipped down to expose several consecutive points. Word strips are placed backward and upside down on the backing and hinged at the bottom with masking or transparent tape. A small piece of adhesive is

FIG. 5—THE HINGED CHART

placed at the top to hold the word strip in place until the appropriate time to reveal it. As points are emphasized, the adhesive at the top is removed and the word strip is flipped down on its hinge, revealing the printed message. Spacing between the word strips should be equivalent to the width of a word strip to avoid overlapping of strips when presentation is made.

FIG. 6—FOLDED WORD STRIP CHART

Folded word strip charts.—The folded word strip chart is a hidden chart on which consecutive word strips folded vertically are unfolded to reveal points in an outline. One half of the word strip is tacked to a backing; then the halves are fastened lightly with a small piece of adhesive. The word strips will fold easily after they are scored lightly with a sharp instrument.

Strip charts.—A strip chart is a hidden chart consisting of points in an outline covered with strips of paper which may be removed to reveal specific points. The strips may be removed

FIG. 7—THE STRIP CHART

completely or allowed to hang by one end to make it easier to make another similar presentation.

Materials for the cover-up strips may be adding machine tape, dry-wall finishing tape (available at lumber stores and builder's supply stores), or strips of cardboard. Even strips of newspaper are perfectly acceptable and are always available. Some teachers use this technique when making a chalkboard presentation.

The Slip Chart.—The slip chart is a hidden chart on which consecutive points are hidden by cardboard strips inserted in channels at the top and bottom. It can be made from a standard church school attendance register. Word strips may be made from adding machine tape and fastened to the register with rubber cement for easy removal.

FIG. 8—THE SLIP CHART

The cover strips may be slipped or pushed out of the channels to reveal consecutive points. The strips should be longer than the width of the chart to make them accessible for easy removal.

Flip Charts

A flip chart is a chart consisting of several bound pages, used for the purpose of making several points by developing them one at a time by exposing a new point on each page. The upright flip chart, inverted flip chart, book-type flip chart and the double inverted flip chart are discussed here.

Any of the flip charts described may be used as picture charts as well as charts using word symbols. The open-book chart is especially adaptable to telling illustrated stories to children. The double inverted flip chart is especially effective when a combination of pictures and word symbols is used.

The upright flip chart.—This chart is a flip chart bound at the top so that consecutive points on single pages can be exposed by flipping the pages up and over. The leaves of the chart may be of thin paper but, if the chart is to stand alone, the front and back covers must be of more rigid construction. Materials may be posterboard, cardboards used by laundries in folding shirts, newsprint, butcher paper, wrapping paper, or pages from the daily newspaper. The want-ad pages of the newspaper are very use-

FIG. 9—THE UPRIGHT FLIP CHART

ful in making flip charts since the background appears to be mottled gray from a distance of eight or ten feet. Guide lines for printing are already on the paper in the form of lines between columns. Plain newsprint can usually be purchased at very low cost at printing shops or at school supply stores. The rolls can be cut to a convenient width with a hand saw.

Top edges of the flip chart may be joined with ring binders, heavy string, masking or transparent tape, or by tacking the pages to the top of a rigid backing.

Inverted flip chart.—This is a flip chart bound at the bottom so that consecutive points on single pages can be exposed by flipping the pages forward. When pages are flipped down, they rest on a table or other flat surface. The nature of the chart eliminates the use of many of the materials which may be used in the upright chart. Newsprint, for instance, does not have enough body to stand upright when the top of the chart is unbound. Cardboard is the most satisfactory material to use. This chart has the advantage of being easy to handle quickly as successive pages are shown. When a page is pulled forward slightly, it falls the rest of the way, taking less time than needed to lift a page up and over. It is necessary to provide a stand-up device of some sort since the chart does not use its two covers as holders.

FIG. 10.—THE INVERTED FLIP CHART

Hinged music tape, available at some music stores, is especially good for fastening the pages of the inverted flip chart together. Ring binders may be used for the same purpose, and in an emergency, coarse string will serve the purpose.

Double inverted flip chart.—Like all flip charts, this chart consists of several pages fastened together at one edge. Its distinguishing feature is that it makes use of both the front and back of the pages. This reduces the cost for materials, for when one sheet is flipped down the size of the presentation surface is doubled. By punching a hole near the top center of each sheet,

FIG. 11.—THE DOUBLE INVERTED FLIP CHART

the chart may be hung on the wall, or on a pencil held in the hand.

Materials for this chart are limited to more rigid types, such as cardboard, since each sheet must have enough body to support itself.

The double inverted chart lends itself to the effective use of illustrations with printed materials. One-half of the presentation surface may be used for an illustration, with the caption on the other half as shown in the illustration.

Open book flip chart.—This chart is similar to other flip charts except it is bound at the side, permitting the pages to be opened like a book.

FIG. 12.—THE OPEN BOOK FLIP CHART

Open book flip charts are especially adaptable to assembly programs which are presented as a unit or in a series. They are attractive when the covers are extended and painted to represent book backs. A ribbon used as a marker between pages improves its appearance. Like the double inverted flip chart, the open book type makes use of both sides of each page.

Single charts and flip charts have been discussed in this chapter. The next chapter describes the construction and use of a wide variety of charts which make use of various adhesive elements in their use and construction.

3

Clingcharts

The term "clingchart" is used to describe charts, boards, or displays which perform the functions of charts but whose component parts adhere to a backing through use of magnetism, friction, static electricty, or other adhesive elements. The term is used instead of other commonly used terms because of its inclusiveness.

Materials used in construction of clingcharts are discussed first in this chapter. A short discussion of the forms of the clingchart and methods for variation of presentation techniques follows.

Materials for Construction

The base of clingcharts may be made from any of several textiles and composition boards. These include burlap, felt, flannel, wool, velour, suede, composition board, unfinished wood, and sandpaper. In the event textiles are used, they must be stretched over a stiff backing.

Burlap clingcharts.—Pleasing textures and a variety of colors are available for construction of these charts. Burlap also has the distinct advantage of being low in price. Components will adhere to it if backed either completely or in spots with wool, flannel, velour paper, or sandpaper. Special materials are available commercially.

Flannel or felt clingcharts.—Felt or flannel is perhaps the best known material used for clingcharts. Smooth texture, variety of color, availability, and ease in handling are advantages of this fabric.

Velour clingcharts.—Velour, though not a textile, is similar in texture to felt or flannel and has unusually good clinging qualities. Some fabrics such as velvet will give the same effect.

Composition clingcharts.—These charts work on the same principle of adhesion as textile or fabric clingcharts. The essential difference is the type of base. Composition boards such as fiberboard have surfaces which have good clinging qualities. Advantages are the ease with which one may be constructed and the low cost. Materials are available at any builder's supply store. Sometimes a small piece may be purchased as scrap material. It is important to select the material with texture in mind. Some composition boards are too smooth. Some, on the other hand, are usable on both sides. Fiberboard, with deep rough depressions, painted white, is perhaps the most acceptable. Adhesives used on the parts can be the same as for textile clingcharts.

Unfinished wood clingcharts.—Few materials serve the purpose better than unfinished wood, which is available at saw mills. Splinters on the surface of the wood cause the components to adhere well.

Forms of Clingcharts

Clingcharts described here are the large folded clingchart, the hand clingchart, the illuminated clingchart, and the single clingchart.

The folded clingchart.—These charts are available at most book and school supply stores, but may be constructed easily by stretching textiles tightly over a rigid backing of heavy cardboard or thin plywood. The two halves may be joined, using a tape hinge, or—when a plywood backing is used—a piano hinge. The chart may be folded for ease in carrying, then unfolded and placed on an easel or table.

The hand clingchart.—This chart is perhaps the most usable of all clingcharts. It is especially adaptable for use in the small Sunday school class or other small groups. It may be constructed like the folded clingchart by using smaller parts. A stiff cardboard file folder, either regular or legal size, is easy to handle and is sturdy. Components are made in the same way as for other clingcharts. Sandpaper strips for hand sanders may be

SANDPAPER
WORD STRIPS

Fig. 13.—The Folded Clingchart   Fig. 14.—The Hand Clingchart

purchased in small lots at a five- and ten-cent store. These strips may be used as word strips without further preparation by writing on the smooth side with crayon or felt-point pen.

Use of this type clingchart makes the presentation more personal and attracts a great deal of attention.

The illuminated clingchart.—For the worker who uses a clingchart often and with large groups, the illuminated clingchart is effective. It is dramatic in appearance and helps make the presentation impressive. The illuminated clingchart uses the same principles in construction as other clingcharts but its base material is limited to textiles. Its chief distinguishing characteristic is that it is illuminated from the back, much like a shadow screen. The light should be subdued to eliminate any unnecessary glare for the group. Its use is more effective when much of the teaching material is symbolic. Use of word strips with the illuminated clingchart depends upon the amount of illumination in the background and in the room.

The illuminated clingchart is constructed as shown in the illustration. The area beneath the fabric must first be covered with wire mesh so that the fabric has a rigid base. The bottom six or seven inches of the presentation surface is covered to prevent direct glare from the light bulb which is placed in the base of the device.

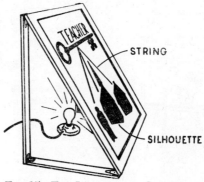

Fig. 15.—The Illuminated Clinghart

Cutout letters, available at many office and school supply stores, have felt-flock backs and may be used when use of words is necessary. Lines used as eye-directors may be made with cotton or wool yarn or soda straws.

The single clingchart.—Charts made from composition boards are generally of this type; however, fabrics may be stretched over

Fig. 16.—Forms of Simple Clingcharts

a single (not folded) piece of rigid backing for a single fabric clingchart. Size or shape of a clingchart is of little consequence; however, a free-form design is attractive when a more dramatic effect is desired. A regular 2:3 or 5:7 ratio is preferable for classroom use. Free-form design is perhaps better for special or unusual meetings.

Magnetboard clingcharts.—These clingcharts use a different principle of adhesion from that characterized by the fabric or

FIG. 17.—THE MAGNETBOARD CLINGCHART

composition clingchart. Metal chalkboards are available at some school supply houses. These are designed for use also as magnetboards. Word strips or symbols are placed on the metal backing and held in place by small magnets. Some manufacturers have recommended standing at a distance and throwing the material at the magnetboard! Such activity only calls attention to the device to the extent that the subject matter is of secondary importance.

One effective use of the magnetboard chalkboard is to use the hidden chalkboard technique described in the chapter on chalkboards. In this technique, magnets hold paper strips over the points in an outline and the strips are removed as points are discussed. A magnet may also be attached to the back of a movable embellishment or indicator such as a pointer or star and moved from point to point in an outline.

The Creative Use of Clingcharts

The unusual adaptability of any form of the clingchart makes it a favorite of the creative teacher.

Embellishments.—Embellishments are components which extend outside or above the main body or base of the chart. As in outdoor posters, an embellishment increases the effectiveness and

Fig. 18.—Embellishments on the Clingchart

attractiveness of the device and gives a three-dimensional effect. Word strips may be extended outside the border of the chart, or movable parts, such as arrows or other indicators, may extend outside the borders of the chart to a predetermined point inside.

Three-dimensional materials.—For the most part, this technique limits materials to those used in simple paper sculpture (folding paper to give a three-dimensional effect). For example, an arrow may be made three-dimensional by folding it down the center and attaching it to a base which is touched with a spot of adhesive. Construction paper, scored with a paper clip, a cuticle stick, or other sharp instrument, is easily folded to give unusual effects. (See Fig. 19.)

The puzzle layout.—Many presentations in education are adaptable to the puzzle layout on the clingchart. A whole item is cut into parts and then fitted together, step by step, on the clingchart. Effectiveness of this type presentation can be increased by using a permanent poster or chart of the same layout. This is especially true if the layout has to be replaced by another one in the series of programs. The permanent poster is helpful in

FIG. 19.—THREE-DIMENSIONAL MATERIALS

preview and review, before and after the puzzle layout is assembled. Pie charts and map puzzles can be used to good advantage as puzzle layouts on the clingcharts.

FIG. 20.—THE PUZZLE LAYOUT

Pictures, mounted on cardboard backed with felt or sandpaper, may be cut into puzzles and assembled on the clingchart. This activity, though especially adaptable to children's groups, is effective for all age groups.

4

Maps

A map is a representation (usually on a flat surface) of the surface of the earth, or of some part of it, showing the relative size and position, according to some given scale or projection, of the parts represented. Geography and history are companions. "His-story" took place in geography. Study and use of maps in teaching can be interesting to both teachers and pupils. The creative teacher can do much more than point to maps mounted on the wall. He can easily adapt them for pupil activity.

In this chapter, maps will be discussed under the classifications of flat maps, relief maps, globes, and chalkboard maps.

Flat Maps

Flat maps for use in religious education are classified here as acetate-covered maps, embellished maps, clingchart maps, floor maps, and duplicated maps.

Acetate-covered maps.—These maps consist of a regular wall map covered with a sheet of acetate. An acetate sheet is either joined at the top, in flip chart form, or fastened at the bottom and any two of the other sides to a backing sheet. The latter construction forms a pocket into which a wall map may be slipped. The acetate sheet serves as a writing surface and enables the teacher to do creative work without damaging the map. A china marking or wax pencil can be used to indicate cities, trace journeys, call attention to specific areas, and so on. The marks

Fig. 21.—Acetate-covered Map

may be erased with a soft cloth or, if the markings have hardened, a cloth moistened with alcohol. A sheet of cellophane can be used instead of acetate but it is not as durable. The pupil may participate in the lesson or program by marking the map either before or during the session.

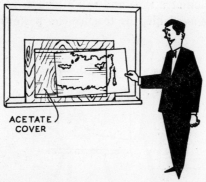

Fig. 22.—Pocket for Acetate-covered Map

Embellished maps.—These are simple wall maps on which points are identified with embellishments such as arrows or circles. These may be cut from colored paper and stuck temporarily on the map with a tiny bit of adhesive. If a metal backing can be

FIG. 23.—EMBELLISHED MAP

provided for the map, it may be used as a magnetboard and indicators can be equipped with a small magnet to provide adhesion.

Clingchart maps.—These maps are especially effective as teaching devices since they permit the teacher or pupil to "build" the map a section at a time and call attention to specific areas. If old maps are available, the teacher can paste them on card-

FIG. 24.—CLINGCHART MAP

board backing, then cut the map into sections and attach adhesive material on the back of each piece. The pieces may then be assembled on the clingchart.

Floor maps.—Such maps are helpful in presenting missionary programs or lessons to a small group. They are enlarged outline maps, traced with crayon, felt-point pen, or other marker, onto large sheets of brown wrapping paper or table cover paper. An opaque projector will facilitate attaining the desired size as well as ease of accurate tracing. The outline is then placed on the floor. Letting the group sit in a circle around the map as the program progresses is an effective teaching procedure. If the map is large enough, members presenting parts of the program may stand near related points on the map. The teacher or leader might choose to indicate specific points with a long pointer as the lesson or program progresses. Accuracy is not all-important. The general impression is the main thing.

Fig. 25.—Floor Map

Duplicated maps.—These maps are outline maps reproduced on a standard duplicating machine. An advantage of this map is that each member of the group may have one. The teacher or leader may suggest that the member or pupil fill in information as it is mentioned in the program or lesson. Such maps are usually used by the pupil, while the teacher or leader uses a large wall map to make explanations. They are helpful in directing the pupil in tracing missionary journeys, locating mission stations, indicating needs of the mission fields, or in simply finding the

FIG. 26.—USING DUPLICATED MAPS

locale of the lesson for the day. Maps should be distributed with a pencil as members assemble, thus creating interest and getting the pupils ready to learn.

Relief Maps

Relief maps are three-dimensional maps which show the configuration of the ground. Such maps may be purchased from a manufacturer or may be made by hand. Or teachers and leaders of younger groups may prefer to build a relief map from clay and sand, letting pupils help in its construction. To conform to three-dimensional specifications, the outline may be made with clay and the interior filled with sand. A variation of this idea is to make the map a "products" map on which actual samples of produce or representative scale models are placed.

Commercial relief maps.—Generally speaking, these maps are too expensive for general church use. However, it may be possible for a church library to add one to its collection of materials and circulate it as it is needed. Some plain, unfinished plastic relief maps of Palestine are available at book stores and are quite effective. Because of their size, their use is generally limited to small classes or groups. They explain many interesting points about Bible lands which are perhaps meaningless otherwise. For example, the term "down to Jericho" has little meaning until a pupil realizes that the road to Jericho was actually a descending road. Also the mystery of the Dead Sea may be explained by showing its below sea-level location.

Handmade relief maps.—Relief maps may be "built" upon an outline map by using paper maché or a thick mixture of 1 part salt, 2 parts flour, and water to moisten. Many mission maps are in outline form and are inexpensive to use as a base. The teacher may make the map or the class or group may do the work as a project. The maps may be kept indefinitely and used again and

FIG. 27.—HANDMADE RELIEF MAP

again. After drying, the maps can be painted with water colors or tempera paints.

Chalkboard Maps

The chalkboard provides a wealth of opportunity for the creative user of maps. Chalkboard maps may be template maps, stencil maps, or permanent outline maps.

Template maps.—A template is a cutout pattern used as a guide for tracing. Usually a handle is placed in the center of the template to make it easy to hold. Templates may be made from heavy cardboard or light plywood. A template of Palestine is simple to make, is easily stored, and because of the nature of Bible study can be used many Sundays throughout the year. The

FIG. 28.—TEMPLATE MAP

template should be held firmly against the chalkboard while the outline is traced with chalk. Fill in the outline with colored chalk to make a more attractive map. Make sure the chalk is not the type which is designed for use on paper. There is a special colored chalk for the chalkboard.

Stencil maps.—Stencil maps are made on the chalkboard from an outline stenciled on a window shade or other thin material. The outline is first traced on the material with pencil, then perforations are made with a pencil point or small hole punch. The

FIG. 29.—STENCIL MAP

stencil is placed over the chalkboard and dusted lightly with an eraser. The outline thus made can be retraced. If the stencil is made on a window shade, it may be installed permanently at the top of the chalkboard and pulled down when needed. A shade will also double for use with the hidden chalkboard technique discussed in chapter 5.

FIG. 30.—PERMANENT OUTLINE CHALKBOARD MAP

Permanent outline chalkboard maps.—Permanent outline maps may be traced with a template or from a pattern projected on the chalkboard with an opaque projector. Instead of chalk, a felt-point pen is used. The nature of the ink in the pen makes a permanent outline which will not erase. Because it is a dark outline rather than a light one, it does not prevent the board's being used in other ways. If the outline needs emphasis, it may be retraced with chalk. If this type map is to be used, it is wise to secure permission from the church building committee or other persons responsible for care of equipment. The teacher or pupil may fill in with chalk the needed information. It may then be erased and the outline used for another lesson or program.

5

Chalkboard

The chalkboard is the "work horse" of teaching aids. Many reasons may be given for its use. Among them are:
1. Chalkboards help to attract and focus attention.
2. Chalkboards are usually available.
3. Chalkboards are adaptable.
4. Chalkboards can be used for development of a logical thought sequence.
5. Chalkboards may be used in such a way as to involve the pupil and his ideas.
6. Chalkboards permit group participation.

Techniques which the creative teacher may develop include the hidden chalkboard, the use of templates, the turnover chalkboard, permanent chalkboard outlines, and stenciled outlines.

The chalkboard is generally used as a chart but because of its distinctive form and composition, it is considered separately.

Chalkboard Techniques

The hidden chalkboard.—The hidden chalkboard technique takes advantage of the element of surprise by attracting attention at the appropriate time, thus deepening impressions. Material which is already visible on the chalkboard as a group assembles tends to lose to some extent its teaching value, except in unusual circumstances when the material is designed to challenge the pupil's thinking ahead of time. There are several techniques which the resourceful teacher may develop and use effectively.

Write information or make a drawing on the chalkboard. Cover it completely with a sheet of cardboard (a discarded pos-

FIG. 31.—HIDDEN CHALKBOARD

ter will do), a window shade fastened to the top of the board, a draw curtain or some similar device. Expose the material at the most appropriate time. If the chalkboard is small and easily handled, material may be written on the board and the board turned backward, then displayed at the proper time.

ADDING MACHINE
OR DRY-WALL TAPE

FIG. 32.—HIDDEN CHALKBOARD USING PAPER STRIPS

For added effectiveness, cover only portions of the chalkboard with paper strips, fastening them to the wooden or metal frame at the edge. Cover the points in an outline in this way and reveal the points in the same manner as described for the hidden chart. Dry-wall building tape, adding machine tape, or similar materials are suitable for cover strips.

The template technique.—Templates are discussed in chapter 4, page 37, as they may be used with maps. Other designs or cutouts may include figures and symbols which may be cut from

FIG. 33.—USING TEMPLATES WITH CHALKBOARD

catalogs, magazines, newspapers, or other publications and used as patterns. They may be pasted on cardboard and then cut out to make a template.

The turnover chalkboard.—Some portable chalkboards are designed so that both sides may be used. The board is placed on an axis so that it may be turned easily to show the reverse side without turning the chalkboard stand around. An example of good usage is to present a question on one side and answer it on the other. For example: "What were Paul's questions at the time of his conversion?" Answers: 1. "Who art thou, Lord?" 2. "What wilt thou have me to do?" Much of the effectiveness of this technique depends upon the teacher's timing in showing the second side.

A word of caution is in order—try out the technique ahead of time to make certain that material on the second side will not appear upside down when the board is turned.

FIG. 34.—THE TURNOVER CHALKBOARD

Chalkboard Designs

Permanent.—Certain designs or symbols may be used frequently enough to merit provision for permanent outlines on the chalkboard. The music staff used in writing music notation may be placed permanently on the chalkboard; however, the use of

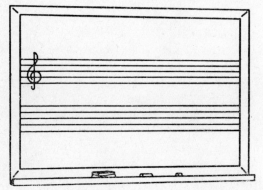

FIG. 35.—PERMANENT CHALKBOARD DESIGNS

the special five-fingered device for drawing the music staff practically eliminates the necessity of having a permanent diagram. The use of the map of Bible lands has already been discussed in chapter 4, page 36. Church recreation leaders will find the permanently painted layouts for basketball and volleyball courts helpful.

Using a felt-point pen or other similar marker with dark ink will result in an outline which cannot be erased but which will not interfere a great deal with use of the chalkboard for other purposes. If white paint is used, the board of course will be unsuitable for other uses.

Semipermanent.—Outlines of a semipermanent nature may be made with a special chalk available at school supply stores.

6

Posters

The essential difference in posters and charts is in their purposes. Posters are not generally designed to convince but to remind; they deliver messages without giving details; they are based on a simplified idea; and they are generally on one sheet only. Thus, many of the "posters" used in religious education are not posters at all, but charts. A poster becomes a chart when it summarizes, compares, contrasts, or performs other services in explaining subject matter.

Posters in religious education are used primarily as reminders of coming events but they can be used effectively as teaching aids. Publicity posters and teaching posters are treated in this

 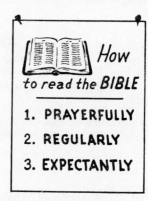

Fig. 36.—Posters and Charts Are Different

chapter. Because of the importance of good design, this chapter
also sets out ten principles of good design.

Publicity Posters

Where "publicity" ends and teaching begins will probably
never be decided. True, publicity posters generally serve the
purpose of announcing the who, what, where, when, and why of
future events. But for a consideration of how this type poster
served a "teaching" purpose, read the following account of the
call of Robert Moffat to the field of missions:

> It was after Robert had left his home in Scotland and begun work
> as a gardener on a large estate at High Leigh, England, that one
> summer evening he set out on foot for Warrington, about six miles
> away, intending to make some purchases in the shops. . . . He crossed
> the bridge that led into Warrington and came to a sudden halt be-
> fore a poster that hung by the roadside. Mastered by a curiosity he
> could not explain, he read the words once and again: "Missionary
> Meeting, Guild Hall, Warrington, Thursday Evening, July 25. Speak-
> er, Reverend William Roby, of Manchester." The date was past, the
> meeting over, and the speaker already departed to his home. What
> invisible hand wove the spell that held young Robert Moffat rooted
> to the spot, oblivious to all around him?
> By a quick process of association the words awakened memories
> that had been for a long time slumbering in the young man's
> mind.

> .   .   .   .

> Then, all at once, he understood why the placard, with its notice
> of a bygone event, stirred such a commotion in his mind. God was
> calling him, Robert Moffat, to the life of a missionary, exactly as he
> had called the men and women of the Moravian church years
> before.[1]

For purposes of this discussion, however, publicity posters will
be considered as those which publicize coming events of the
church calendar. Teaching posters will be considered those which
are used purposefully in a formal teaching-learning situation with

---

[1]Ethel Daniels Hubbard, *The Moffats* (New York: Friendship Press,
1944), pp. 21-23. Used by permission.

teacher and pupil. Publicity posters will be classified as **single** posters and multiple posters.

Single publicity posters.—Single posters are printed on one side only. Though they may appear in multiples in display, the individual poster is still printed on one side only.

Double posters.—Double posters are designed to take advantage of economical production by printing the layout on both sides of the poster board.

Three or four posters stapled together at the sides to make a three-sided or four-sided device is attractive and has the advantage of readability from all directions. Uses of these devices are many. They may be placed on the tables used at fellowship dinners. They may be stacked in totem-pole fashion to attract further attention. They may be placed on turntables singly or stacked. They may be stacked in succession on the floor of hallways.

FIG. 37.—STAND-UP POSTER MADE FROM THREE SINGLE POSTERS

A stand-up poster can be made from two single posters stapled at the top to make a back-to-back device which will support itself. It is effectively used on tables and in displays and may be read from opposite directions. If left standing too long it will flatten out, unless it is fastened to the support or joined with a third strip at the bottom.

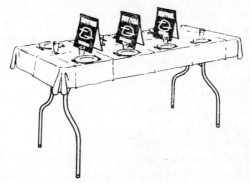

FIG. 38.—STAND-UP POSTER MADE FROM TWO SINGLE POSTERS

If posters are ordered from a printer, an 11 by 14 size is economical, since four posters may be cut from a standard poster sheet 22 by 28. Once the type is set, the additional cost is small. As many as 100 of these identical posters can be used effectively in an average church to publicize one event. A good principle to follow is to place the posters at any spot where people are likely to be.

Display

Suggested display methods for single posters include their use on stairway treads, as three-sided or four-sided devices, and as

FIG. 39.—SERIES OF SINGLE POSTERS ON RISERS

double stand-up posters. A series of identical posters placed on the risers on a stairway attract attention and do a good selling job.

FIG. 40.—DOUBLE POSTER ON DOOR GLASS

For good publicity, double posters may be placed on glass doors so they are visible from two directions.

One of the most effective display methods for double posters is to attach them perpendicularly in a series to a series of door facings at about eye level. The series makes an impact and has the advantage of being read from both directions as people pass up and down the halls.

FIG. 41.—DOUBLE POSTERS ON DOOR FACINGS

Another display method makes use of a simple 2 by 2 by 4 inch holder which has been slit one inch deep across the top side. The poster is set in the slot and may be displayed singly or in a series on dining tables or hallway floors.

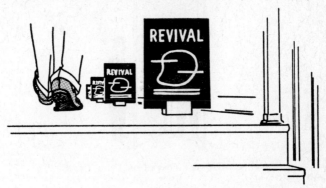

Fig. 42.—Double Posters on Simple Block Stand

Teaching Posters

Posters lend themselves to effective teaching procedures. They are best used in resource centers in assembly programs, in the classroom, or for general display (on bulletin boards) as reminders.

Posters for resource centers.—Usually a chart is used for the resource center but posters are effective, since one of the purposes of the assembly program resource center is to draw attention to a particular subject and not necessarily to give details of the subject.

Posters in resource centers will be more attractive if placed in a picture frame. An old frame may be painted and kept for such purposes. A cardboard frame may be made from the patterns given in chapter 7.

When a poster is used in the resource center, caution should be taken not to employ too many other objects in the same center. If many objects are necesary, perhaps they themselves should

FIG. 43.—SINGLE POSTER IN FRAME

constitute the resource center with simply a placard or streamer carrying whatever word thought is necessary. It is not at all necessary to use a "softly draped cloth" or a candle or a vase of flowers in the resource center to dramatize the appearance of the poster, although sometimes effectiveness is increased by the use of them. When the display becomes stereotyped by using these materials then the teacher, leader, or director should rethink his purposes.

Posters for the classroom.—Teaching with charts is usually done in the classroom. However, posters too may be used with good results. Like charts, posters may be used in a series or may be hidden until proper timing calls for display. Other effective display techniques may also be employed.

Principles of Design for the Amateur

The principles are outlined to help the amateur avoid some of the most common pitfalls in poster and chart design. These principles are rather elastic, but generally they will result in more attractive and usable posters.

Select a pleasing size and shape.—As discussed in chapter 2, the most pleasing proportion is 2 by 3 or 5 by 7. The creative teacher, however, need not be bound by these proportions if the situation calls for other shapes.

Include one basic idea.—Since a poster is to be only suggestive, it becomes confusing when two or more suggestive ideas are incorporated in the same design. If more ideas are necessary, a series of posters should be used.

Design the layout with "eye-direction" in mind.—Arrows and ellipses are simple eye-directors. The expert artist can achieve eye-direction in many ways but for the amateur it is advisable

FIG. 44.—"Z" DESIGN IN A POSTER

to arrange material in the basic "Z" or "S" or reverse "S" or the "C" or reverse "C" design. Note how the design in the Figure 44 illustration follows the "Z" design.

Use one basic attention-getter.—After this part is decided upon, the rest of the poster should be developed in relation to it. Added interest is achieved when the attention-getter or eye-catcher is three-dimensional or is used as an embellishment.

Limit the number of styles of lettering.—For the amateur, the use of over two styles of lettering results in unattractive work. These styles may be varied in size, for special effects and attractiveness will still be maintained. Use of color will also vary the effect of the same letter style.

Try to master two styles of lettering.—One simple style of block lettering and script lettering or handwriting can be effectively combined. Many different lettering books are on sale at schools and art supply stores.

Limit colors to two in addition to the background color.—The three colors should make a pleasing combination. One of the colors may be a darker shade of the background to avoid likelihood of clashing colors. Some effective color combinations are:

Light blue background with dark blue and peach or shades of red

White background with black and any other color

Black background with pastel combinations

Yellow background with brown and red combination.

Leave plenty of blank space.—Filling too much of the space is perhaps the most dangerous pitfall for the poster maker. Blank space should be left around all sides and as much as possible incorporated in the design.

Break the monotony of the background.—Again, the expert artist may not need to do this. The amateur can improve his work, however, by breaking the monotony of the background in one of the following ways: a spattered area in one of the basic colors, a connector line in the background, a "blurb" or free form design in a contrasting color, etc. A border of broken lines is effective and easily achieved.

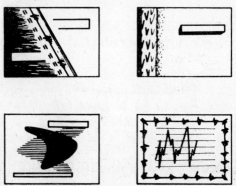

FIG. 45.—BREAK THE MONOTONY OF THE BACKGROUND

Use posters to suggest rather than tell all.—This can be accomplished by using such techniques as initial letters of a commonly used place or organization, or using a design which suggests a person, place, or thing. If the poster tells all, the teaching effectiveness is lessened since the pupil is not led to concentrate on the material.

Avoid the use of "puns" and minimize the play on words.— Such copy as " 'Leaf' us all study the program this week" is neither funny nor effective. It is a type of promotion which is not becoming to the serious purposes of religious education. Moreover, such a play on words says nothing. The viewer is apt to remember the play on words and forget the message. Humor is good and can be effective in poster design but its use requires much more skill than the average teacher or poster maker possesses. In this respect, teachers could well heed the advice of those familiar with writing advertising copy:

> Cleverness, as it is executed in practice, is usually mediocre or low-grade in quality. It often is not really clever; it is would-be cleverness that fell flat. It frequently has no clear, unmistakable meaning for the reader. Sometimes it is irrational and absurd.
>
> Whether well executed or not, cleverness always is distracting. It diverts the mind from thoughts about the product or message.[1]

FIG. 46.—GOOD USE OF HUMOR IN POSTERS

---

[1]Merrill DeVoe, *Effective Advertising Copy* (New York: Macmillan Co., 1956), p. 214.

Humor or a clever idea used in such a way as to drive home a legitimate point or to suggest a frame of mind or circumstance in which the viewer occasionally finds himself, will sometimes prove effective. Figure 46 shows good use of humor. It attacks a prevalent excuse among potential Bible school workers and does it in a humorous way. The viewer immediately associates himself with the problem presented.

7

Special Devices

Special devices are sometimes created for special purposes or used when a lack of materials or other emergencies make it necessary. The needs of a teaching situation may dictate the creation of a special device. Among these are shadow screens, picture-frame boards, accordian-fold story boards, resource centers, and other materials which are purely creative and defy classification.

Shadow screens.—A shadow screen is an impressive variation for use in teaching. It is especially adaptable to large groups.

The shadow screen consists of a transluscent material such as muslin cloth or tablecloth paper stretched over a frame. A light placed to the rear of the screen casts the shadow of any object or person appearing between the screen and the light. The "picture" may move but, generally, still pictures are best.

Using people for the shadows requires practice. Some principles to remember are: (1) Keep the characters near the screen (about 1 inch away) to make a clearcut, natural sized image. The farther away the light is from the screen, the farther the characters may be from the screen. (2) Let the characters use symbolic properties such as a telescope to indicate a look into the future or a Bible to suggest devotional activities. (3) Rehearse again and again so that the viewer does not see the changes in scene. A curtain in front of the screen or a rheostat on the light will facilitate efficient scene changes.

The use of characters may be combined with symbols. If characters are used, the screen should be at least six feet six inches

FIG. 47.—LARGE SHADOW SCREEN

tall and approximately five or more feet wide. A frame of two by two's joined with angle irons is usually sturdy enough. The screen may, however, be large enough to accommodate several persons; or, it may be a simple framed shadow box, using cutouts to tell the story. The latter is readily adaptable to assembly program presentations and use with smaller groups.

FIG. 48.—SHADOW BOX SHADOW SCREEN

Three-dimensional display frames. Attractiveness of displays is greatly increased by the use of three-dimensional frames. These

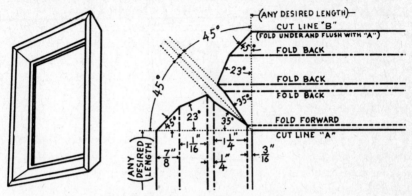

FIG. 49.—PATTERN FOR CARDBOARD FRAME

may be cut and folded from the poster board itself and painted with spray paint or a brush. The corner design shown here may be used on a standard size (22 by 28) poster sheet and still have a poster approximately 15 inches by 21 inches. If frames for larger posters are desired, the design may be placed under an opaque projector and increased in size as needed.

The related resource center.—Occasionally the teacher may want to display objects, charts, or posters in a related resource center. This center is generally called an "interest center." The term "related resource center" carries several connotations, making it preferable to the old "interest center" idea. First, it suggests a relationship to the subject at hand. Secondly, it suggests not only a relationship but it suggests that the material is to be *used* as well as seen.

The related resource center may be varied by using a "growing resource center." One object, poster, or chart may be used during the first lesson in a unit, and related materials may be added during succeeding lessons. This technique makes review an easy matter.

Display boards.—A display board is a learning aid consisting usually of a rigid backing on which related objects, embellishments, charts, posters, or a combination of these elements may be displayed for the purpose of improving a teaching-learning situation. The display board is sometimes referred to as a bulletin board. The term "display board" is used here because "bulletin board" usually is used to describe an area in a public building reserved for the posting of bulletins or news items of an unrelated nature.

Display boards may be made of cork, fiberboard, peg board, and other suitable materials.

Objects may be easily displayed on the type of display board which consists of three-fourths inch plywood backing in which one-half inch holes have been drilled about six inches apart. Six-inch dowel pins inserted into the holes are strong enough to hold movable shelves on which objects may be displayed. These boards may be mounted on picture rails and moved as the need arises.

FIG. 50.—ACCORDION-FOLD STORY BOARD

Accordion-fold story boards.—Pieces of cardboard may be hinged with music tape, masking, or transparent tape to create a folding story board similar to the illustration. Butcher paper or other similar material may be folded in the same manner. If the teaching situation calls for an aid which shows progression a step at a time, this device will serve the purpose.

This device is also effectively used with the opaque projector, since it unfolds as parts are inserted and can be folded up as it leaves the projector.

An interesting variation of the folding story board is the three-dimensional story board. This, of course, leaves the realm of simple teaching aids, but is mentioned because of its relatedness. These may be made from shallow boxes (such as hose boxes) after reinforcement with balsa wood or similar material. This aid can be used to good advantage with elementary groups when actual objects need to be used in telling a story. The method of assembly is shown in the illustration. Use library book tape to make the bindings more permanent.

THREE-DIMENSIONAL
STORY BOARD

FIG. 51.—THREE-DIMENSIONAL STORY BOARD

The three-dimensional story board may also be used in classes or groups where collections of materials are made, and may be used with the opaque projector to show images of actual objects. The objects may be twice as deep as one section of the board since two sections fold together. If used in an opaque projector, it is best, however, to limit the depth of the object to the depth of one section.

8

Simple Teaching Aids
in Unit Procedure

In education, a "unit" is a body of content related in its parts and related in the whole to preceding and succeeding parts. Thus, units usually consist of from two to five or more lessons or programs which are individually related in their parts and as a whole are related to preceding and succeeding programs. Occasionally a unit may consist of only one lesson or program.

Why Are Lessons and Programs Planned by Units?

The unit plan is necessary because of the time limit for study in religious education. Generally, a thorough exploration of material is not possible in one session. The unit plan provides time for development as well as presentation of ideas.

The unit plan makes it possible for lesson development to change direction slightly as individuals participate and inject feelings and information.

The carry-over impact of the lesson to lesson procedure improves learning and makes teaching easier.

Through preview and review, a relating of materials is made possible.

Interest and anticipation on the part of the learner is developed.

Properly relating the parts of a unit to each other in the minds of the learners and making the learner conscious of a continuing emphasis is one of the most neglected, yet one of the most necessary, features of creative teaching. The resourceful teacher can do much with the devices described in preceding chapters to develop this feeling of continuity.

How Can Simple Teaching Aids Be Used to Increase Effectiveness of the Unit Procedure?

The teacher himself (or the pupils) may want to develop a device to be used with the unit, planning to use the review and preview technique as the unit progresses.

In the case of program building where leaders or captains are in charge on alternate Sundays, leaders may collaborate at the beginning of a unit to develop a device which will be used by both workers throughout the unit.

What Are Some Principles to Follow in Selecting Simple Learning Aids?

The principle of relatedness.—The device or learning aid should relate the programs or lessons to the unit theme and to each other. This may be done by presenting the related titles of the programs (see Fig. 4, p. 18). It may also be accomplished by presenting the aims of different lessons or programs, and reviewing and previewing them as the unit progresses. The use of appropriate learning aids helps the teacher or leader to properly relate the parts as a unit.

The principle of appropriateness.—The learning aid should be appropriate to the particular unit. The teacher should ask, "Which of all these possibilities will be most helpful in meeting the objective or aim?" He must frankly answer such questions as, "Will a mimeographed sheet serve the purpose of this program better than a hinged chart or a clingchart?"

Units of study in religious education are generally related to one of the basic areas of study, such as evangelism, Christian fellowship, world missions, the church, denominational life, doctrines, development of the spiritual life, stewardship of life, the Bible, and Christian morality. A learning aid designed to accompany a unit on the Bible might be more adaptable to the open book chart (Fig. 12) than would a unit on Christian citizenship, for example. The use of a map would be more appropriate in tying together a unit on world missions than a unit on courtship, marriage, and the Christian home.

The principle of availability.—A learning aid should be readily available or easily constructed. Suggestions outlined in previous chapters have been made with this principle in mind. Many materials which are already available around the home or the church have been suggested: shirt boards, adding machine tape, the newspaper, shoe polish daubers, and other simple materials.

The principle of variety.—Keeping a simple check list of learning aids used will assist the teacher in planning for variety in each unit. The strip chart (Fig. 7) might conceivably be used in some way for all units, but that is not necessary. Following the principle of appropriateness will largely take care of variety.

The principle of stimulation.—The teacher should plan for stimulation or anticipation on the part of the learner. Many of the learning aids illustrated in previous chapters may be used in such a way as to focus attention upon one part of a unit or lesson at a time. At the same time, the learner knows from the construction of the learning aid that other points or ideas are to be presented.

The principle of preview and review.—In work on closely related units, it is especially important to the learner that the principle of preview and review be used by the teacher in planning and presenting the lesson. Learning becomes more effective when the learning period is extended with preview and review. Many learning aids are adapted to the retention of emphases found in all parts of a unit and simply have to be preserved and used for recall. When it is difficult or time-consuming to provide review with such learning aids as the clingchart puzzle, it is advisable to construct a permanent aid containing the same material. Most charts are designed for easy use in preview and review.

The principle of simplicity.—The simplest learning aid available which can carry or impress a truth adequately should be chosen. The chalkboard, though the simplest of all learning aids in general use, is many times the most effective and adaptable. It is almost always available. If its use will insure the success of the presentation, then a more complicated device is not necessary. In fact, the more complicated aid might even lessen the impact.

Conclusion

Through these pages, an effort has been made to present ideas and describe devices which can be put into use with a minimum outlay of money, time, and materials. Teaching materials come in strange forms, are where one finds them, and many of them cost no more than yesterday's newspaper. It is hoped that the teacher and leader, through a study of these pages, may discover that simple learning aids can be effective "tools for teaching."